Presented to

....

By

....

Time with God for Mothers

© 2011 by Jack Countryman

Published in Nashville, Tennessee, by Thomas Nelson. Thomas Nelson is a registered trademark of HarperCollins Christian Publishing, Inc.

Thomas Nelson titles may be purchased in bulk for educational, business, fund-raising, or sales promotional use. For information, please e-mail SpecialMarkets@ThomasNelson.com

Cover and interior design by Koechel Peterson Design, Minneapolis, MN

ISBN-13: 978-1-4041-8951-5

Printed in the United States of America

16 17 18 19 WOR 9 8 7 6 5

Time with God
FOR
Mothers

BY JACK COUNTRYMAN

J COUNTRYMAN®

A Division of Thomas Nelson Publishers
Since 1798

Table of Contents

New Beginnings

Therefore, if anyone is in Christ,
he is a new creation; old things
have passed away; behold, all
things have become new.

2 CORINTHIANS 5:17

HOW WONDERFUL TO READ the word *anyone* in the Scripture text. No one is exempt. Everyone in Christ is included, and the love of God has forgiven all our sins and shortcomings. Old things that haunt our past have been forgiven. We have become brand-new in Christ, to live with joy in our hearts as children of a loving and caring heavenly Father. Therefore, let each day be filled with the presence of our Lord as we live for His glory.

A Mother's Prayer

The LORD is near to all who call upon Him,
To all who call upon Him in truth.
He will fulfill the desire of those who fear Him;
He also will hear their cry and save them.

PSALM 145:18–19

LORD, TO KNOW THAT YOU are ever near to me when I call upon Your name is both comforting and reassuring. May I always call upon You in truth. Protect my heart from any fears that take me away from Your everlasting love. May You always be the desire of my heart. May I live each day with purpose and with a joyful gladness that only You can supply. May I forever praise You. Amen.

God Bless Our Home

Blessed be the God and Father of our Lord Jesus Christ, who has blessed us with every spiritual blessing in the heavenly places in Christ.

EPHESIANS 1:3

THE HOME IS THE CENTER of everything that makes the life of a Christian family complete and meaningful. When we live for Him, our home will be blessed. Putting Christ first in our lives will cause us to be more aware of the abundance He bestows on us. Let Christ be ever-present, to comfort and strengthen the bond that can never be broken through Him.

The Love Relationship with God

> And we have known and believed the love that God has for us. God is love, and he who abides in love abides in God, and God in him.
>
> 1 JOHN 4:16

WHEN WE DISCOVER THE LOVE that only God can give, everything in life changes. He loves us so much that He is willing to accept us just the way we are—warts and all. His love covers all our shortcomings, and we do not have to earn the love that He so generously gives us. When we accept His offer to abide in His love, we abide in God and He is forever with us in every circumstance of life—and nothing or no one can take that away from us. Praise God!

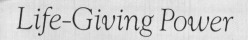

Life-Giving Power

This is my comfort in my affliction,
For Your word has given me life.
PSALM 119:50

SOMETIMES LIFE IS DIFFICULT. We face many challenges and disappointments that we may find hard to accept. But fortunately we have a heavenly Father who cares deeply for us in every way. He has given us His Word to guide us and give us the wisdom to withstand any situation that life brings. We only have to open the Book of Life to find comfort that allows us to be all that God wants us to be for our benefit and His glory.

God's Treasure

"They shall be Mine," says the LORD of hosts,
   "On the day that I make them My jewels.
   And I will spare them
   As a man spares his own son who serves him."

MALACHI 3:17

WE ARE GOD'S TREASURES, and He has declared that we are His jewels. Often we may not realize that, to God, we are more precious than diamonds, rubies, or gold. Each one of God's children is a treasure that is more meaningful to Him than anything we could ever imagine. Therefore, let each day be filled with His love as we receive the blessing God so generously wishes to give.

Facing Difficult Times

And we know that all things work together for good to those who love God, to those who are the called according to His purpose.

ROMANS 8:28

O N THIS SIDE OF HEAVEN, we will never understand how "all things" can work together for good for God's children. We recognize that not all things in themselves are good, but God knows the ultimate outcome, and we can trust Him in all our circumstances. When facing difficult times, lean on the Lord for strength, courage, and the will to handle the challenges of life. Keep in mind, "If God is for us, who can be against us?" (Romans 8:31). Nothing can ultimately triumph over us, for in the end, God always wins and we win with Him.

A Time for Worship

God is Spirit, and those who worship Him must worship in spirit and truth.

JOHN 4:24

GOD DESIRES FOR EVERY MOTHER to worship Him. He actively seeks those who will worship Him according to the truth of the Scripture and by the power of the Holy Spirit. When you worship God in spirit and in truth, you will experience a sense of refreshment in your own spirit. Worshiping Him satisfies your very being, and it helps build intimacy in your relationship with Him.

God's Absolute Possibility

But Jesus looked at them and said to them,
"With men this is impossible, but with
God all things are possible."

MATTHEW 19:26

So many times in life we fail to realize that all things are possible through God. He is the God of absolute possibilities. When you choose to honor God, live for Him, and serve Him with all your heart, you can find true contentment. Psalm 37:4 says, "Delight yourself also in the LORD, and He shall give you the desires of your heart." When you spend time with God and He becomes an important part of your life, He places within your heart the desire to honor Him and bring glory to His Holy name. Praise God!

The Trust of God's Goodness

And God will wipe away every tear from their eyes; there shall be no more death, nor sorrow, nor crying. There shall be no more pain, for the former things have passed away.

REVELATION 21:4

WHAT A WONDERFUL PROMISE God has given each of us. We can look forward to being with our Lord and Savior, and we can celebrate His love, which is everlasting. Whatever trials we face or whatever seemingly impossible problems we encounter, God assures us that we can trust in His goodness and grace. Therefore, let us rejoice in all of our circumstances and praise God for the gift of a new life in Him, which He has generously given us.

The Best Is Yet to Come

But as it is written:
"Eye has not seen, nor ear heard,
Nor have entered into the heart of man
The things which God has prepared for
those who love Him."

I CORINTHIANS 2:9

LIFE IS FILLED WITH MANY challenges and opportunities. You work hard to provide the best for those you love and care about. But how many times do you stop and remember that the best is yet to come? God is preparing a better life for you. He only asks that you love Him and "trust in the LORD with all your heart" (Proverbs 3:5a).

The Joy of a Mother's Faith

For whatever is born of God overcomes the world. And this is the victory that has overcome the world—our faith.

1 JOHN 5:4

THE GIFT OF FAITH HAS BEEN given to every mother who loves the Lord with all of her heart. Jesus expects you to grow in your faith, to trust in Him, and to depend on Him to help you overcome the difficulties and challenges you face. Jesus said in Matthew 17:20, "If you have faith as a mustard seed . . . nothing will be impossible for you." So let the joy of the Lord spring from your lips, and praise the Lord for His many blessings.

God's Comfort

Cast your burden on the LORD,
And He shall sustain you;
He shall never permit the righteous to be moved.

PSALM 55:22

When David wrote this psalm, he penned for you an outline of God's desire for you. The Lord wants very much for you to cast all of your burdens upon Him. He is willing, and He is able to sustain you in every circumstance of life. When you love and worship the Lord, He will enable you to handle anything that may come against you. He will never run out of mercy, love, or grace.

The Sound of His Voice

My sheep hear My voice, and I
know them, and they follow Me.

JOHN 10:27

GOD'S SPIRIT WISHES TO SPEAK to your spirit, if you will but take the time to listen to the sound of His voice. He has promised to sustain you and give you eternal life. There is nothing or no one that can take that away from you. You belong to God, and He wants very much to be involved in every area of your life—to guide you, comfort you, sustain you, and give you the peace that passes all understanding. What a wonderful Savior is Jesus our Lord!

God's Gift of Love

ALL WE HAVE TO DO TO RECEIVE God's love is
to confess with our mouths and believe in
our hearts that Jesus died for our sins. Everything
we do and don't do, face and don't face is touched
by His continuing love. Everything about us
hinges on unconditional love because God, who
is love, created us in His image. God helps us
grasp His Word, not merely so that we can gain
knowledge, but so that we can come to know,
love, obey, and enjoy the God of the universe.

He Carries Our Burdens

For My yoke is easy and My
burden is light.

Matthew 11:30

A MOTHER'S LIFE IS SELDOM EASY. You carry a
large responsibility in your family. When
you walk with God, He promises that His
burden is light and His yoke is easy. Being in
right standing with God is essential. Jesus said
that those who abide in Him, draw near to
Him, listen to His Word, and obey His commands would bear "much fruit" (John 15:5).
Let Jesus carry your burdens, and enjoy the
fruits of walking with Him.

The Joy in Jesus

Now may the God of hope fill you
with all joy and peace in believing,
that you may abound in hope by the
power of the Holy Spirit.

ROMANS 15:13

G OD DESIRES FOR EVERY MOTHER to experience
the hope, joy, and peace that only He can
give. As you grow in the Spirit, God wants you to
experience more of those gifts. Let each day be filled
with the power and presence of the Holy Spirit. Let
the glow of the Holy Spirit flow through you that
others might see the joy of Jesus in your life. Walk
with God, and you will have the opportunity to
share His love.

Wait on the Lord

Wait on the LORD;
Be of good courage,
And He shall strengthen your heart;
Wait, I say, on the LORD!

WAITING IS NOT A VERY POPULAR WORD in the life of most people in our culture. We want everything . . . now, but God has promised that He will act on our behalf when we wait for Him. Many times we choose not to wait; instead, we run ahead of Him and try to fix things on our own. If we will only wait on the Lord, He promises to strengthen our hearts and give us the courage to wait for His answers. Seek His strength today.

God's Sufficient Supply

And my God shall supply all your need according to His riches in glory by Christ Jesus.

PHILIPPIANS 4:19

SOMETIMES IT IS VERY HARD TO comprehend that God's grace is sufficient for all our needs. John tells us that without Jesus we can do nothing (John 15:5), but with Him all things are possible. Every mother experiences certain demands and stresses in life that can seem overwhelming. But praise God, Jesus has promised to supply all our needs according to His riches in glory.

Lord, Wipe Away All Tears

He will swallow up death forever,
And the Lord GOD will wipe away tears from all faces;
The rebuke of His people
He will take away from all the earth;
For the LORD has spoken.

ISAIAH 25:8

THIS IS A PROMISE THAT THE LORD gives to us. Whatever we truly need, He will provide. He gives strength to the weak, shelter to the homeless, shade to those fainting in the scorching sun, comfort when life seems unfair, and joy when we walk closely with Him. The Lord will wipe away our tears and give us a new heart, because He loves us and we are most precious in His sight.

When a Miracle Is Needed

Then He took the five loaves and the
two fish, and looking up to heaven,
He blessed and broke them, and gave
them to the disciples to set before
the multitude.
LUKE 9:16

H OW MANY TIMES HAVE WE SAID to God,
"I need a miracle"? A child is sick, a bill
can't be paid, a job is lost, or any number of
things can happen to make life seem impossible. Jesus demonstrated to His disciples and
to the multitude who needed something to
eat that through Him all things are possible.
When life throws you a curve, run to God.
His Spirit is willing, and your miracle may be
just around the corner.

The Solution to Sin

But now in Christ Jesus you who once were far off have been brought near by the blood of Christ.

EPHESIANS 2:13

SIN SEPARATES US FROM THE LOVE of God. In sin, we selfishly want to live our own way and never consider the consequences of life without God. The beautiful thing about God is that He looks beyond our sin and openly seeks to forgive us if only we will ask for His forgiveness. God created us to enjoy an intimate relationship with Him, and He offers redemption and salvation to us for the same reason. He yearns for that close fellowship with us that was made possible through the death and sacrifice of Jesus.

Healing for a Broken Heart

The LORD is near to those who have a broken heart,
And saves such as have a contrite spirit.
Many are the afflictions of the righteous,
But the LORD delivers him out of them all.

PSALM 34:18–19

"SOMEONE REALLY LOVES YOU" are words that each of us wants to hear when we have been disappointed and our hearts have been broken. God loves us with an everlasting love, and when life seems impossible, He is always near to comfort, strengthen, and walk with us through whatever disappointments we may face. The Lord will never leave us. Open your heart and let the love of God flow over and through you.

Serving Others with Joy

And let us not grow weary while doing
good, for in due season we shall reap if
we do not lose heart.
GALATIANS 6:9

DELIGHT AND FULFILLMENT go hand-in-
hand as a mother seeks to find purpose in
the responsibility of serving her family. She is the
center of the home, and God has given her the
unique ability to create an atmosphere of peace
and joy that only she can bring. Let the joy of
the Lord fill your countenance so that what you
portray may be contagious to everyone you in-
fluence and come in contact with daily. You are
God's gift to those you love.

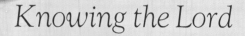

Knowing the Lord

I will instruct you and teach you in the
way you should go;
I will guide you with My eye.

PSALM 32:8

ONE OF THE SECRETS OF LIFE is to always remain teachable. Growing in Jesus Christ is a process that God has promised to lead us through when we open our hearts and seek His guidance daily. God wants us to know Him, and He has promised to teach each of us in the way we should go. Isaiah 30:21 says, "This is the way, walk in it." Let each day be filled with the power of God's Spirit, that He might give wisdom and understanding, so that our lives may be everything God has planned.

A Life Lesson

You did not choose Me, but I chose you and appointed you that you should go and bear fruit, and that your fruit should remain, that whatever you ask the Father in My name He may give you.

JOHN 15:16

JESUS DOES NOT WANT ANY OF US to lead unproductive or unfocused lives. He chose us not only for salvation, but also to play a significant role in His kingdom. He wants each of us to fulfill a particular purpose for our success and for His glory. We have been designed to bear much fruit and, when our lives are filled with His purpose, we can do all things through Christ because we will have His strength. Let each day be filled with joy because we are children of the King.

Finding Confidence in God Alone

> For every house is built by someone, but He who built all things is God....but Christ as a Son over His own house, whose house we are if we hold fast the confidence and the rejoicing of the hope firm to the end.
>
> HEBREWS 3:4, 6

WHEN GOD IS YOUR CONFIDENCE, you can rely on Him. As a mother, you are required to do many things for your family. Trusting in God is the first step you must take if you wish to be all that God wants you to be. When you learn to rely on God's Spirit and diligently seek His wisdom, God will supply you with all the confidence you will ever need. Let nothing or no one take that away.

Walking in His Word

Now this is the confidence that we have in Him, that if we ask anything according to His will, He hears us. And if we know that He hears us, whatever we ask, we know that we have the petitions that we have asked of Him.

1 JOHN 5:14–15

Love for God is not merely a warm sentiment or a pleasant feeling. It is a living, active force that changes who we are. Jesus Himself forever connected love for God with love for people. Let each day be filled with the hunger to know more of God's Word. Let it guide you to live with joy in your heart and a burning desire to be filled with the wisdom that is given when we walk in God's Word.

The Trust Only God Can Give

In You, O LORD, I put my trust; let me never be put to shame. For You are my hope, O Lord GOD; you are my trust from my youth. Let my mouth be filled with Your praise and with Your glory all the day.

PSALM 71:1, 5, 8

SURRENDERING TO GOD BRINGS a certain trust that only He can give. This is the foundation that breaks down the barrier we often have before we come to know Him. When we openly express our love for God and the faith we have in Jesus Christ, we are willing to praise Him. Expressing faith and trust in the Lord will create a natural desire to share Him with others.

May the Lord Be Praised Forever

Because Your lovingkindness is better than life,
My lips shall praise You.
Thus I will bless You while I live;
I will lift up my hands in Your name.
My soul shall be satisfied as with marrow and fatness,
And my mouth shall praise You with joyful lips.

PSALM 63:3–5

PRAISING THE LORD IN ALL of life's situations is a habit that we all need to apply to our lives. It is a healthy expression of God's never-ending love for each of us. Through our praise and His Spirit, God gives us the ability to face whatever life may bring. God truly wants the best for us. When we praise Him, the sense of security that only He can give will fill our hearts and minds and give us the peace that passes all understanding.

Living in the Spirit

But if the Spirit of Him who raised Jesus from the dead dwells in you, He who raised Christ from the dead will also give life to your mortal bodies through His Spirit who dwells in you.…the Spirit Himself bears witness with our spirit that we are children of God, and if children, then heirs—heirs of God and joint heirs with Christ, if indeed we suffer with Him, that we may also be glorified together.

Romans 8:11, 16–17

JESUS PROMISED US A COMFORTER, the Holy Spirit, to be with us always and give life to our mortal bodies. With that promise, we are heirs of God and joint heirs with Christ. We are in God's family, and no one or nothing can take that away from us. Life may bring certain challenges and times of suffering, but the rewards that have been promised are greater than we can possibly imagine. Therefore, we should celebrate the love of God and let His Spirit be alive in all that we do each day.

The Essence of Prayer

Call to Me, and I will answer you, and show you great and mighty things, which you do not know.

Jeremiah 33:3

Throughout the Bible, God promises to speak to each of us, but we must listen for His voice. To listen actively, we must come before the Lord with expectation in our hearts, eagerly anticipating Him speaking to us. This is the essence of prayer. The conversation we have with God in prayer will bring comfort. God is waiting day and night to listen and speak to our hearts. He is just a conversation away. We can talk to Him because He loves us so very much.

When Trouble Knocks
at Your Door

Beloved, do not think it strange concerning the fiery
trial which is to try you, as though some strange thing
happened to you; but rejoice to the extent that you
partake of Christ's sufferings, that when His glory is
revealed, you may also be glad with exceeding joy.

1 Peter 4:12–13

IN THE LIFE OF A MOTHER, you can count on trouble to
come knocking at your door. No one is exempt, and
life has a way of bringing trials that test your family. The
Scripture speaks openly about such trials. You have been
commanded to rejoice in those situations so that your
commitment to Christ may be strengthened and God's
glory may be revealed. Open your heart and mind to
Him, and trust in His plan for your life. Your ability to
use these trials as building blocks strengthens your home
so that it cannot be destroyed.

Obeying Your Word

Whoever comes to Me, and hears My sayings and does them,
I will show you whom he is like: He is like a man building a
house, who dug deep and laid the foundation on the rock. And
when the flood arose, the stream beat vehemently against that
house, and could not shake it, for it was founded on the rock.

LUKE 6:47–48

JESUS IS THE ROCK AND FOUNDATION for everything
you will need in your Christian life. When you choose
to build your family on the rock of God's Word, you
can face whatever challenges life brings. You can trust
in the Word of God to protect, guide, and deliver you
through life's problems and those circumstances beyond
your control. Stand firm and let God's Word direct you
in all things because He wants the very best for you and
those you love.

When Adversity Is Near

My soul, wait silently for God alone, for my expectation is from Him. He only is my rock and my salvation; He is my defense; I shall not be moved. In God is my salvation and my glory; The rock of my strength, and my refuge, is in God.

PSALM 62:5-7

WE CAN TRUST THAT THE Rock of God goes before us, inviting us to hand over our troubled emotions to Him. If we look for Him, He will be there. Sometimes it is extremely hard to wait on God, particularly when we face certain challenges that require us to make difficult decisions. But no matter what we face, God is our greatest defense.

Patience that Comes from the Lord

> My brethren, count it all joy when you
> fall into various trials, knowing that the
> testing of your faith produces patience.
> But let patience have its perfect work,
> that you may be perfect and complete,
> lacking nothing.
>
> JAMES 1:2–4

PATIENCE IS A VIRTUE that we all have to learn. Although no one longs for trials to come, God uses those trials and sufferings to build our faith and to teach us patience. A mother learns, through time, that patience has rewards, especially when she sees her children grow into what God wants them to be. "Let patience have its perfect work, that you may be perfect and complete, lacking nothing."

Resting in God

But those who wait on the LORD
Shall renew their strength;
They shall mount up with wings like eagles,
They shall run and not be weary,
They shall walk and not faint.

ISAIAH 40:31

AS A MOTHER, YOU MAY OFTEN FIND the many responsibilities that fill your daily life overwhelming. Sometimes you may wonder, *Will things ever get better?* The best thing you can do is relinquish your concerns to the Lord. He is the One who has the power to bring all matters to their proper perspective. When you try to handle problems by yourself, you can become weary. God does not want you to run yourself into exhaustion; instead, He desires that you rest in Him.

Finding True Contentment

Now godliness with contentment is great
gain. For we brought nothing into this world,
and it is certain we can carry nothing out.
And having food and clothing, with these
we shall be content.

I TIMOTHY 6:6–8

OUR SOCIETY SEEMS TO FOCUS on worldly
contentment, striving to gain material
things, money, or position. Growing true contentment comes when we trust God to be our
sole provider. The Scripture reminds us that
"we brought nothing into this world, and it is
certain we can carry nothing out." Contentment will come when we learn to express grati-
tude for what we have. God has blessed His
children with so much, why not take inventory
of your blessings and give thanks to God? Our
greatest source of contentment is Jesus Christ.
Let each day be filled with His presence.

Seek His Guidance

Trust in the LORD with all your heart, and lean not on
your own understanding; in all your ways acknowledge
Him, and He shall direct your paths.

PROVERBS 3:5–6

GOD'S GUIDANCE IS MORE THAN SUFFICIENT for all the tests or trials we may face. God has promised, "You will seek Me and find Me, when you search for Me with all your heart" (Jeremiah 29:13). He loves us unconditionally. He yearns for us to come to Him with an open heart and to find the joy and peace that only He can provide. Continually seek His guidance for your life as you lean on Him.

Giving to Others

Give, and it will be given to you: good measure, pressed down, shaken together, and running over will be put into your bosom. For with the same measure that you use, it will be measured back to you.

LUKE 6:38

GOD WILL INSTILL WITHIN YOU a desire to reach out and give generously of your time and love to others if you ask Him. When you give to others, God, in return, gives back to you generously the love, joy, and comfort that only He can give. The giving mother will have a glow that is contagious and a joy that will infect everyone that she loves and encounters. You are God's ray of sunshine.

A Season of Grace

And He said to me, "My grace is sufficient for you, for My strength is made perfect in weakness." Therefore most gladly I will rather boast in my infirmities, that the power of Christ may rest upon me.

2 CORINTHIANS 12:9

GOD'S GRACE—THESE ARE TWO of the most powerful words in the Bible. Those words cover our mistakes and shortcomings. They give us hope to look beyond life's disappointments. Adversity is a bridge to a deeper relationship with God. He does not glory in our pain or sorrow, but He does use our experiences to teach us about His love and faithfulness. God knows the future. He understands the benefit of our shortcomings and how they can be used to strengthen our faith, refine our hope, and settle our hearts into a place of contentment and trust. God has promised that His grace is sufficient, and He will walk with us through the valley times of life.

A Mother's Gift

As each one has received a gift, minister it to one another, as good stewards of the manifold grace of God. If anyone speaks, let him speak as the oracles of God. If anyone ministers, let him do it as with the ability which God supplies, that in all things God may be glorified through Jesus Christ, to whom belong the glory and the dominion forever and ever. Amen.

I Peter 4:10–11

YOU HAVE BEEN BLESSED with certain gifts and talents. How you use those gifts and talents will reflect on the life you choose to lead and whether or not you imitate the love that God so generously gives. The Christian life is meant to be a fruitful and joyful experience. It takes a conscious, deliberate, Spirit-filled action to develop the gifts God has given. What gift has God given you? Enjoy the blessings of that gift as you walk with Him every day.

Encouragement Changes Everything

Rejoice with those who rejoice, and weep with those who weep. Be of the same mind toward one another. Do not set your mind on high things, but associate with the humble. Do not be wise in your own opinion.

ROMANS 12:15–16

EVERYONE NEEDS TO FEEL SPECIAL. A mother's love and encouragement deeply impacts her children and nurtures their self-esteem. The Bible invites you to "Rejoice with those who rejoice, and weep with those who weep." Rejoicing and weeping are both heartfelt emotions. Sharing them with your children and your family creates the kind of deeply felt connection that happens only when you choose to get involved in the lives of those you love. The time a mother spends encouraging her loved ones creates a strong bond and mirrors for them the love of God.

Strength in Times
of Trouble

I will love You, O LORD, my strength.
The LORD is my rock and my fortress and my deliverer;
My God, my strength, in whom I will trust; My shield
and the horn of my salvation, my stronghold.

PSALM 18:1–2

WHERE DO WE RUN WHEN trouble knocks on the door? The Bible reveals to us that the Lord is our strength, rock, fortress, and deliverer. He is also described as our shield and the horn of our salvation. If we fill our minds and hearts with the realization that God cares about everything that goes on in our daily lives, then He is ever-present to strengthen and encourage us for our benefit and His glory. Confrontation and trouble are inevitable, but God is faithful. We can count on Him, for He is sufficient.

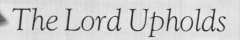

The Lord Upholds

The steps of a good man are ordered by the LORD,
And He delights in his way.
Though he fall, he shall not be utterly cast down;
For the LORD upholds him with His hand.

PSALM 37:23–24

GOD HAS PROMISED THAT WHEN we walk faithfully with Him and when He becomes an integral part of our everyday lives, His spirit will guide us in such a way that His protection will surround everything we say and do. Though we would like to be perfect, the truth is that we make mistakes, we fall down, and we become a disappointment to ourselves and those we love. God wants to take us gently by the hand and lead us, so that we are blessed and He is glorified.

The Power of Forgiveness

Let all bitterness, wrath, anger, clamor, and evil speaking be put away from you, with all malice. And be kind to one another, tenderhearted, forgiving one another, even as God in Christ forgave you.
EPHESIANS 4:31–32

WHEN WE ALLOW A BITTER SPIRIT to lodge in our souls, it becomes both painful and destructive. An unforgiving heart lies at the root of many physical, emotional, psychological, and spiritual problems. Through Jesus Christ we are forgiven and, therefore, we are directed to forgive those who offend us. Hurt in life is unavoidable, but no pain is too deep or too widespread to lie beyond the power of God's forgiveness. Rely on God's power when dealing with forgiveness. When you do, it will bring freedom to your life.

The Blessing of Serving Others

And He sat down, called the twelve, and said to them, "If anyone desires to be first, he shall be last of all and servant of all."

MARK 9:35

A MOTHER'S LIFE IS FILLED with serving others. Family members receive a blessing from a mother's care. Putting others first involves listening to and hearing what your loved ones really need. When you serve others, you will become a living example of God's love and the kind of person God desires for you to be.

God's Word Is Alive

For the word of God is living and powerful, and sharper than any two-edged sword,
piercing even to the division of soul and spirit,
and of joints and marrow, and is a discerner
of the thoughts and intents of the heart.

HEBREWS 4:12

ONE OF THE GREATEST CHALLENGES we
face in our Christian lives is the need to
read and meditate on God's Word. The Bible
is not dead; it lives because God brought it
into existence and because the Spirit of God
brings its message to live in our hearts. God's
Word has the power to change our lives.
Let each day be filled with God's presence
through His Word, so that you may receive
the knowledge, wisdom, and understanding
so essential for your spiritual life.

Father Knows Best

Therefore do not be like them. For your Father
knows the things you have need of before
you ask Him.

MATTHEW 6:8

PRAYER IS ESSENTIAL IN THE LIFE OF A MOTHER. It is
your opportunity to praise your heavenly Father, to
confess sin, and to ask God for His forgiveness. Prayer is
a way to draw attention to how much you need God. We
all need to know and love God in a deeper way. Com-
municating with God about the details of your life will
open your heart to His love and help you recognize your
dependence on Him. The more prayerful you become,
the deeper your love for God will grow.

The Peace of God Passes All Understanding

Be anxious for nothing, but in everything by prayer and supplication, with thanksgiving, let your requests be made known to God; and the peace of God, which surpasses all understanding, will guard your hearts and minds through Christ Jesus.

PHILIPPIANS 4:6–7

GOD WANTS EACH OF US TO HAVE the peace in our hearts that "surpasses all understanding." When we take our concerns to God, He has the power and wisdom to take care of them because He always has our best interests at heart. When our prayer life includes every area of our lives, we open heaven's door and allow God to be ever-present. Through our prayers and thanksgiving, we allow God's peace to guard our hearts and minds.

God Promises a New Heart

I will give you a new heart and put a new spirit within you; I will take the heart of stone out of your flesh and give you a heart of flesh. I will put My Spirit within you and cause you to walk in My statutes, and you will keep My judgments and do them.

EZEKIEL 36:26–27

SOMETIMES OUR HEARTS FEEL BROKEN when we experience disappointment with someone or with certain events. But realize that God will never disappoint us. God does not want to remodel our hearts; He wants to give us brand-new ones. He places His Spirit within us to lead us to do His will. He wants us to experience transformation, not mere accommodation. Let each day be filled with the joy that only comes from God.

When I Miss the Mark

For all have sinned and fall short of the glory of God, being justified freely by His grace through the redemption that is in Christ Jesus.

ROMANS 3:23–24

THE GUILT THAT SIN BRINGS into our lives is often the stumbling block that keeps us from a deeper walk with God. God stands ready and willing to forgive us when we miss the mark and repent of our sin. God's love is unconditional, overwhelming, and abundant. Through His forgiveness, He wants us to learn from our mistakes and grow to be more like Jesus. We are not perfect, but our heavenly Father looks beyond our mistakes and calls us to a deeper walk with Him for our benefit and His glory.

The Blessing of Life in Jesus

I am the door. If anyone enters by Me, he will be saved, and will go in and out and find pasture. The thief does not come except to steal, and to kill, and to destroy. I have come that they may have life, and that they may have it more abundantly.

JOHN 10:9–10

THE BEAUTY OF THIS PASSAGE IS that Jesus is not one of many doors to the Father, but the *only* door. He never claimed to be one route among several to an intimate relationship with God; rather, He made it clear that He is the only way. When He is our Savior, the life He has planned for us is filled with abundance. God truly wants for us a life filled with purpose, joy, and happiness through a close, personal, intimate relationship with Him.

Be Still

> God is our refuge and strength, a very present help in trouble....Be still, and know that I am God; I will be exalted among the nations, I will be exalted in the earth!
>
> Psalm 46:1, 10

WHAT A COMFORT TO KNOW that God is your refuge and strength. Some days as a mother, you may feel as if your world has been shaken and everything you depend upon has been cast into the sea. But if you put your hope in God, you have no need to fear, because you have a refuge that can never be moved. God asks you to "be still and know that I am God." There are times when God will display His glory in blinding flashes impossible to ignore. But most times, you will meet Him in the quietness of your heart.

A Godly Mother

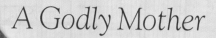

And whatever you do, do it heartily, as to the Lord and not to men.

COLOSSIANS 3:23

BEING A MOTHER IS A great responsibility. And it begins not with your children, but with allowing the Holy Spirit to guide you in all that you do. As a Christian, you are called to be dependent on God for how you live and the decisions you make. As a Christian mother, that calling is so much greater, as you are responsible not only for putting God first in your own life, but also for leading your children to do the same. Being a godly mother does not come easily; it can only be accomplished when Jesus leads the way. Invite Him to be a part of every decision you make and every child you nurture.

God's Presence

Now may the God of peace Himself sanctify you completely; and may your whole spirit, soul, and body be preserved blameless at the coming of our Lord Jesus Christ.

1 THESSALONIANS 5:23

WHEN YOU THINK ABOUT GOD being ever-present in your life, it is often hard to imagine. Life is filled with everyday problems and responsibilities, but when you choose to open yourself to His love and let Him be a part of all that you say and do, He promises to be ever-present. The Holy Spirit has been given to you as a gift to "comfort your hearts and establish you in every good word and work" (2 Thessalonians 2:17), to give you the strength and courage to be all that He wants you to be.

God's Dwelling Place

> Or do you not know that your body is the temple of the Holy Spirit who is in you, whom you have from God, and you are not your own? For you were bought at a price; therefore glorify God in your body and in your spirit, which are God's.
>
> 1 Corinthians 6:19–20

Thanks to Jesus' sacrifice, your body is now God's home. When you have guests in your home, you honor them by putting things in order and doing all that you can to make them feel comfortable. By taking care of yourself physically, mentally, and spiritually, you are doing the same for God. You are giving your heavenly Father a warm welcome home. Your body is a sacred place where God's Spirit dwells. How you treat yourself is a reflection of the kind of dwelling place you desire to offer the Father who loves you.

Being Daily Filled with the Lord

Come to Me, all you who labor and are heavy laden, and I will give you rest. Take My yoke upon you and learn from Me, for I am gentle and lowly in heart, and you will find rest for your souls. For My yoke is easy and My burden is light.

MATTHEW 11:28–30

WHAT A WONDERFUL INVITATION that God gives to each one of us! What mother doesn't need rest and relaxation from all that she is required to do? God's desire is for you to share the burdens you carry so that you might be the mother He wishes for you to be. He promises to be gentle and to humbly refresh and restore your weary soul. Let God fill you with His presence every day.

Resist the Devil

Therefore submit to God. Resist the devil and he will
flee from you. Draw near to God and He will draw
near to you. Cleanse your hands, you sinners; and
purify your hearts, you double-minded.

JAMES 4:7–8

HUMILITY IN CHRIST WILL ENABLE YOU to overcome
your human tendencies toward worldliness—tendencies that draw you away from Him. Turn away from
the evil one as he has no place in your home. You are
asked to, "Draw near to God," and you are promised that
"He will draw near to you." You are encouraged to take
the first step in your relationship with your heavenly Father. He waits patiently for you to come to Him with an
open heart. Live each day with this purpose in mind: to
please God and to bless those whom God has given you
to nurture and love.

Desire God

And having food and clothing, with these we shall be content. But those who desire to be rich fall into temptation and a snare, and into many foolish and harmful lusts which drown men in destruction and perdition. For the love of money is a root of all kinds of evil, for which some have strayed from the faith in their greediness, and pierced themselves through with many sorrows.

I TIMOTHY 6:8–10

WHEN YOU DESIRE GOD, you spend your time and energy getting to know Him better and doing what pleases Him. Pursuing riches more vigorously than a relationship with God will lead you to sorrow. Instead of focusing on money, focus on God. Thank Him for how He has blessed you, and share what He has so generously given. You will find yourself rich in joy and contentment.

Let Go of the Past

Brethren, I do not count myself to have apprehended; but one thing I do, forgetting those things which are behind and reaching forward to those things which are ahead, I press toward the goal for the prize of the upward call of God in Christ Jesus.

PHILIPPIANS 3:13–14

LET GO OF THE PAST. Don't try to live in yesterday. God wants your life today and every day in the future. Someone has said, "Make today the first day of the rest of your life." Let God, who loves you with an everlasting love, be the One you turn to for strength, wisdom, patience, and the self-control you need to be a blessing to those God has given you to love.

My Heart's Desire

Delight yourself also in the LORD, and He shall
give you the desires of your heart.
Commit your way to the LORD, trust also in
Him, and He shall bring it to pass.
PSALM 37:4–5

WE HAVE AN OPEN INVITATION
from God to delight ourselves
in Him. We do that by spending time
with, learning about, and loving the
One who cares for us. When we learn
to let the Word of God be a part of our
lives, He will place within our hearts
the desire for a closer walk with Him.
We will be blessed when we trust in
God's faithfulness.

The Love that Never Goes Away

For God so loved the world that He gave His only begotten Son, that whoever believes in Him should not perish but have everlasting life.

JOHN 3:16

JESUS CHRIST LOVES YOU with a love that has no end; it is complete. His love is unconditional; you can't earn it, work for it, be good enough to have it, or convince God that you deserve it. No matter how great your sacrifice, it can never compare to the sacrifice Christ made for you. Because He was willing to give His life that you might have everlasting life, nothing is more important than the life of Christ within you. Let His love flow from you to those around you.

Seek His Wisdom

See then that you walk circumspectly, not as
fools but as wise, redeeming the time, because
the days are evil. Therefore do not be unwise,
but understand what the will of the Lord is.

EPHESIANS 5:15–17

WHEN GOD INVITED SOLOMON to ask for whatever
he wanted, the king requested wisdom (1 Kings
3:9). That God-given wisdom taught Solomon that only
a fool tries to solve problems without God's help. In a
mother's life, tests and trials come in all shapes and sizes.
You must come to God for wisdom and understanding.
The wisest approach to life's challenges is to seek God
for His plan and direction. When you meditate on God's
Word, you will gain insight by studying the Scripture
and its truth. Difficult decisions become easier to handle
when God is the One guiding you.

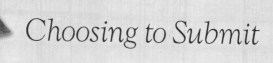

Choosing to Submit

Submitting to one another in the fear of God.
EPHESIANS 5:21

WHEN JESUS COMES INTO OUR LIVES, His Spirit lives within us to guide us and bring glory to His holy name. Verse 21 refers to submitting—that does not mean to be under the absolute control of another, but rather to voluntarily place yourself under the authority of another. When we choose to submit to God's will and walk in the power of His Spirit, He is willing and ready to bless our lives.

Freedom in Christ

Then Jesus said to those Jews who believed Him, "If you abide in My word, you are My disciples indeed. And you shall know the truth, and the truth shall make you free."

JOHN 8:31–32

To the believer, these verses are considered the emancipation proclamation. But freedom in Jesus does not always come easily. Your personal response to Jesus' commands determines whether you will be able to live in the freedom of your salvation. A person in prison can receive a signed pardon and the warden can unlock the jail door, but that person has to put one foot in front of the other and walk outside. When you obey God, you can count on Him to reveal exciting new things. The key to crossing the bridge between belief and experience is obedience. You must take the step of faith and live for Him.

A Work in Progress

Therefore, as the elect of God, holy and beloved, put on tender mercies, kindness, humility, meekness, longsuffering.

COLOSSIANS 3:12

SOMEONE HAS SAID, "A mother's work is never done." As children develop and you nurture and raise them to adulthood, you learn how to teach and guide them. In your spiritual life, God is also transforming you. He wishes you to dwell on the things of God rather than on things of the flesh. When you give God the priority in your life, those around you will be touched by God's love, kindness, and mercy. God has given you a special task, to live each day in His fullness.

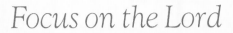

Focus on the Lord

"And you shall love the LORD your God with all your heart, with all your soul, with all your mind, and with all your strength."
This is the first commandment

MARK 12:30

IN THE SPORTS WORLD, some say, "focus is the name of the game." When you concentrate on developing your natural skill and work hard toward perfection, you become the best athlete you can be. In your spiritual life, when you are focusing on the Lord and when living for Him is your number one priority, the life that you lead will be filled with the presence of God. He has promised to give you all that you need to live a fruitful, productive life—and God will never break that promise.

Walking with God

For the Scripture says, "Whoever believes on Him will not be put to shame."...For "whoever calls on the name of the Lord shall be saved."

ROMANS 10:11, 13

ANYONE WHO PUTS THEIR FAITH in Jesus Christ will receive eternal life. The Christian life is filled with blessings and promises for every mother that only God can give. People that you meet in life may disappoint you, but God, in His love and mercy, merely asks you to accept the gift of salvation. Everything you need to know about your salvation is found in God's Word. God blesses you when you hear His promises and respond to them in faith.

Faith Is the Key

But without faith it is impossible to please Him, for he who comes to God must believe that He is, and that He is a rewarder of those who diligently seek Him.

HEBREWS 11:6

FAITH IS NOT WISHFUL THINKING or believing what you know isn't true. Instead, it is the conviction that God will always do what He promises to do, regardless of the circumstances. Faith proclaims the trustworthiness of God and His complete and willing ability to do what we cannot. Do not place confidence in yourself. Philippians 4:13 says, "I can do all things through Christ who strengthens me."

Be Brand-New Every Day

Therefore we do not lose heart. Even though our outward man is perishing, yet the inward man is being renewed day by day.

2 CORINTHIANS 4:16

SOCIETY IS FILLED WITH programs, articles, and advertisements telling us how to stay young, lose weight, and be more desirable, and eternal optimism keeps us striving to achieve those things. Thankfully, God offers us a better hope than this. With God, we will grow older and better. Despite the emphasis modern culture places on youth, a person whose self-esteem and self-identity are rooted in a relationship with God is a person who can age with dignity and grace. If we invite God's Spirit to live in us, then our spirit will be made brand-new every day.

Love and Respect Are True Partners in Marriage

Nevertheless let each one of you in particular so love his own wife as himself, and let the wife see that she respects her husband.

EPHESIANS 5:33

IN THE BOOK, *Love and Respect*, the author brings to light the fact that every woman wants and needs love from her husband. Through this love, she has the desire to be the best helpmate and mother she can possibly be. The husband, in turn, essentially needs the respect of the one he has chosen as his partner in life and marriage. When love and respect become fruitful, working partners in marriage, the couple becomes open to the opinions and desires of one another. God has established a plan for marriage. Let His love and Spirit be the center of your family. He has promised His blessing and just reward.

What Is Your God-Given Talent?

For the kingdom of heaven is like a man traveling to a far country, who called his own servants and delivered his goods to them. And to one he gave five talents, to another two, and to another one, to each according to his own ability; and immediately he went on a journey.

MATTHEW 25:14–15

IT HAS BECOME POPULAR IN OUR CULTURE for people with little to great talent to audition in hopes of obtaining a career in the entertainment world. In these competitions, there are many who audition and compete, but only one who wins the prize. God, on the other hand, has given each of us great talents to use for His glory, and He has promised the prize of heaven to all those who are faithful to Him. What is your talent? Discover and develop your God-given talent and allow it to become all that God wishes for your life.

The Lord Is There

Where can I go from Your Spirit? Or where can I flee from Your presence? If I ascend into heaven, You are there; if I make my bed in hell, behold, You are there. If I take the wings of the morning, and dwell in the uttermost parts of the sea, even there Your hand shall lead me, and Your right hand shall hold me.   PSALM 139:7–10

HAVE YOU ASKED YOURSELF, "Why would God want to communicate with me?" The truth is, as followers of Christ, we are all saved by grace, sanctified and washed, saints and children of the living God. God sees us as children who need to listen and receive guidance every day. God loves us just the way we are. He knows our weaknesses, sinful desires, and transgressions; and, yet, He longs to have an intimate relationship with us. Even with all of our baggage, we are a permanent part of His family.

Forgiveness Is a Priceless Gift

As far as the east is from the west,
So far has He removed our transgressions from us.

PSALM 103:12

BECAUSE GOD IS PERFECT and will not accept sin, He has graciously given you the blessing of forgiveness when you miss the mark and disappoint Him. God wants every part of you—body, soul, mind, and spirit—to grow closer to Him and enter into a joyful relationship with Him. You must accept God's precious gift of forgiveness when you make mistakes that separate you from God. Confess your sin and ask for His forgiveness. He will forgive, forget, and never again remind you of your shortcomings. Praise God!

The Holy Spirit

> But the fruit of the Spirit is love, joy,
> peace, longsuffering, kindness, goodness,
> faithfulness, gentleness, self-control.
> Against such there is no law.
>
> GALATIANS 5:22–23

THE CLOSER YOU GET TO SOMEONE who truly walks in the Spirit, the better they look. They radiate integrity. You may find that you open up to them in an uncharacteristic way. When you walk in the Spirit, everything will grow and flourish, and the fruit of the Spirit will change the way you interact with others as you take on those characteristics. The fruit of the Spirit is a true indication of your dependence and sensitivity to the prompting of the Spirit. To live the Christian life is to allow Jesus to live His life in and through you.

Security in Jesus

The LORD shall preserve you from all evil;
He shall preserve your soul.
The LORD shall preserve your going out and your coming in
From this time forth, and even forevermore.

PSALM 121:7–8

GOD HELPS, PROTECTS, and guides those who seek Him with all their hearts. He never promises that this life will be free of hardship or pain, but He insists that for those who know and love Him, their soul shall be preserved. God surrounds those who love Him, like a thick wall surrounding an ancient city. He covers us on every side so that nothing reaches us without first passing through His loving hands, which is the best security system ever created.

A Mother's Character

And not only that, but we also glory
in tribulations, knowing that tribulation
produces perseverance; and perseverance,
character; and character, hope.

ROMANS 5:3–4

WHEN YOU BECOME A MOTHER, you automatically assume the responsibility of someone other than yourself. From that moment on, building blocks are created that will gradually form the character of the mother you will become and the children you will raise. Adversities are God's way of maturing you into a person who looks more like His Son. No one likes trials and suffering, but because of your faith, you may begin to understand how God can use them for your good and His glory. He yearns for you to be more like Him, so that you may live with a joy in your heart that will last forever.

Beauty that Will Last Forever

While we do not look at the things which are seen,
but at the things which are not seen. For the things
which are seen are temporary, but the things which
are not seen are eternal.

2 Corinthians 4:18

WHEN WE THINK OF BEAUTY, we look in the mirror and reflect on what we see. Eventually, the outward beauty we possess will change and fade away. But the beauty that will last forever comes from the inside as God changes our priorities, allowing us to become more like Him. If we love the Lord, we will make it our aim and our delight to please Him by the way we live. We should look for ways to make Him smile. Let your light so shine that others will see the gift of His love, which is a beauty that will be eternal.

Patience Is a Gift from God

He who is slow to anger is better than the mighty,
And he who rules his spirit than he who takes a city.

PROVERBS 16:32

EVERY MOTHER NEEDS PATIENCE. You are the anchor of your family, but raising children can test your patience. In James 1:4, the Scripture tells us, "Let patience have its perfect work, that you may be perfect and complete, lacking nothing." Without patience, you may react to stressful situations with anger and emotion. God wants the gift of His patience to help everyone in your family gain a sense of how precious a mother's love is for those she cares for every day.

Let Jesus Live in and Through You

I will meditate on Your precepts,
And contemplate Your ways.
I will delight myself in Your statutes;
I will not forget Your word.

PSALM 119:15–16

LIVING FOR JESUS IS A full-time experience. Many Christians have never experienced the power and encouragement available to them through memorizing Scripture. When we lock portions of God's Word in our minds and hearts, they remain available to help strengthen us in difficult times. The more we allow the Word to be a part of our lives, the more we grow spiritually. God has given us the sword of the Spirit, which is the Word of God. Let Jesus come alive to us through His Word.

God Knows What You Need

"Have I not commanded you? Be strong and of good courage; do not be afraid, nor be dismayed, for the LORD your God is with you wherever you go."

JOSHUA 1:9

A MOTHER'S LIFE IS FILLED with challenges that often make life less than pleasant. You do the best you can and deal with those situations that need to be solved. In the midst of all of this, God knows exactly what you need. When you invite God into your daily life and depend upon His Spirit for wisdom, He has promised to give you the answers you need and the ability to take care of whatever life brings your way. Listen to His still, small voice; His guidance for you is closer than you can imagine.

God's Plan

Let us hold fast the confession of
our hope without wavering, for He
who promised is faithful.

HEBREWS 10:23

GOD IS AWARE OF EVERY SITUATION you encounter, and He can fit them all into the master plan of your life. You live in a world where problems and difficulties happen daily. But no matter what happens, God promises to use your experiences—even the tragedies—for a redeeming purpose. He is Lord of your life, both during the good days and in the bad moments. Today, no matter what life throws at you, rest in the promise and the hope that God can use any situation to create the beautiful tapestry of your life.

Loyalty Is a Choice

But Ruth said:"Entreat me not to leave you, Or to turn back from following after you; For wherever you go, I will go; And wherever you lodge, I will lodge; Your people shall be my people, And your God, my God."

RUTH 1:16

OUR RELATIONSHIP WITH GOD is usually reflected in our relationships with other people. The more loyal we are to God, the more loyal we tend to be with friends and family members. God wants us to remain loyal to Him, to our family, and to others He puts in our lives. Loyalty comes from the heart. It is motivated by a love that wants the best for the other person. Loyalty also demands trust. When someone is loyal to another, their relationship is strong and deep. Loyalty is not built around circumstances; popularity, or convenience; it is built on devotion to God and love for those we care about.

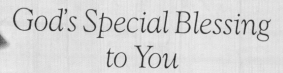

God's Special Blessing to You

And I will bless her and also give you a son by her; then I will bless her, and she shall be a mother of nations; kings of peoples shall be from her.

GENESIS 17:16

MANY MOTHERS WANT A SPECIAL blessing from God. They ask for something they really want. Have you thought about giving God the opportunity to bless you the way *He* wants? Sarah, Abraham's wife, at ninety years of age had never had a child. She had probably prayed for children. But God's timing is always perfect. The unexpected blessing came—God offered a son. God had promised Abraham he would be the father of many nations. God's blessing was far better than the blessing sought by Sarah. If you look to the Lord, your blessing will come according to His plan for your life.

The Lord's Servant

Then Mary said, "Behold the maidservant of the Lord! Let it be to me according to your word." And the angel departed from her.
LUKE 1:38

MARY TRUSTED GOD AND WAS A GOOD and faithful servant. She was a young girl when she learned she was to become the mother of Jesus. She was engaged to Joseph and her life was following the course she expected when God asked her to do something unbelievably difficult. Mary was an ordinary girl with extraordinary godly character and an uncommon faith. She provided a model of inspiration for ordinary women. She lived her life in relative obscurity; yet, the world has celebrated her obedience to God for nearly two thousand years. God may ask you to do things that seem impossible. But as you trust Him, you will find that He will walk with you through all situations.

Anger and Listening Are Like Oil and Water

So then, my beloved brethren, let every man be swift to hear, slow to speak, slow to wrath; for the wrath of man does not produce the righteousness of God.

JAMES 1:19–20

HAVE YOU EVER FELT ANGRY over bad treatment? What truth might get rid of the anger you feel? James gave three guidelines for anyone who feels the sting of anger. First, be willing to listen. Give the person you're angry with a chance to defend themselves and explain their actions. Second, be "slow to speak." Meditate and look at the situation from all angles before you respond. And lastly, be "slow to wrath." Calm yourself; seek self-control with the help of the Holy Spirit. If you follow these practical steps when you feel angry, you will become aware of the love God wants you to share with others.

A Mother's Sacrifice

I beseech you therefore, brethren, by the mercies of God, that you present your bodies a living sacrifice, holy, acceptable to God, which is your reasonable service.

ROMANS 12:1

WHAT DOES IT MEAN TO BECOME a living sacrifice, holy and acceptable to God? Paul wrote to the Roman believers to encourage them to give themselves to God. Personal sacrifice is a voluntary action. The best way to worship God is by giving yourself to Him each and every day, and asking Him to use you for His glory. You make this sacrifice by making a simple request. Ask Him to work in your life, to lead you, to empower you. When you live for Him, a new energy and enthusiasm will flood your heart, and a desire to get involved for the glory of Jesus will grip your life.

Experience Is a Wonderful Teacher

"For My thoughts are not your thoughts, nor are your ways My ways," says the LORD. "For as the heavens are higher than the earth, so are My ways higher than your ways, and My thoughts than your thoughts."

ISAIAH 55:8–9

EXPERIENCE IS A TERRIFIC TOOL, but no matter how much experience, knowledge, and understanding you have about life, you will still fall short of God. He is on a higher plane; His thoughts are not the same as yours. When you see the world around you and the challenges it brings, God sees beyond them. You can trust God and turn to Him when you need someone whose knowledge is all encompassing. God promises to come through in your life in a way that is best for you.

A Mother's Love Transforms

And do not be conformed to this world, but be transformed by the renewing of your mind, that you may prove what is that good and acceptable and perfect will of God.

ROMANS 12:2

GOD WANTS YOU TO DEPEND ON His Spirit, to be transformed into a person who loves Him and wants to please Him through willing obedience. This transformation begins in your mind. God can make you a new and different person. Paul said we shouldn't be conformed to or live in harmony with the world; rather, we should be "transformed" by the renewing of our minds. You are renewed by giving your life—your habits, your thoughts, your words—over to God. You commit yourself to listening to Him and seeking what He wants for you. Day by day, God's Spirit works in your heart to transform you into someone more like Him.

Mothers' Prayers
in the Bible

HAGAR: Genesis 21:16–19

HANNAH: 1 Samuel 1:10–11, 27–28; 2:1–10

LEAH: Genesis 29:31–35

MARY: Luke 1:46–55

NAOMI: Ruth 1:8–9; 2:20a

RACHEL: Genesis 30:22–24

SYROPHOENICIAN MOTHER: Matthew 15:22–28

ELIJAH ON BEHALF OF ZAREPHATH WIDOW: 1 Kings 17:17–22

The Responsibilities of Motherhood

COMMITMENT: 2 Kings 4:30; Psalm 37:4–6; Proverb 16:3;
Isaiah 49:15–16

COMFORT: Isaiah 66:13; 2 Corinthians 1:3–5

COMPASSION: Exodus 2:6–10; Proverbs 31:20; Ephesians
4:32; Philippians 2:1–3; Colossians 3:12–13; 1 Peter 3:8

DISCIPLINE: Proverbs 29:15, 17; 2 Timothy 2:24–26

EXAMPLE: Proverbs 31:30-31; Titus 2:3–5, 7; 1 Peter 3:3–6

FAITH: Exodus 2:3; Ruth 2:12; Matthew 15:28; 17:20–21;
Mark 11:22–23

GODLINESS: Proverbs 31:10–12, 30; Luke 1:41; 1 Timothy
2:10; 4:7

HOME: Proverbs 31:17–18, 27; Titus 2:5

INTERCESSION: 1 Kings 17:13–14; Matthew 15:22–28

LOVE: 1 Corinthians 13; Titus 2:4; 1 John 4:7–11; 2 John 4–5

MORALITY: Judges 13:4; Proverbs 31:10–11, 29; Luke 1:6; 1
Timothy 2:15; Titus 2:5

OBEDIENCE: Genesis 7:7; Deuteronomy 26:16; 1 Kings 17:13–
15; Psalm 119:112; Luke 1:38; 17:32–33; 1 Peter 3:6

PRAYER: Psalm 54:2; Matthew 6:5–6, 33; 7:7–8; Mark 11:24–26

PROVISION: Exodus 2:3–8; 1 Samuel 2:19; Proverbs 31:13–16, 19; Luke 2:7

SACRIFICE: Genesis 3:16; 1 Samuel 1:10–11, 22–28; Luke 1:38; Colossians 3:18; Hebrews 13:15–16; 1 Peter 3:1

THANKFULNESS: 1 Samuel 2:1; 1 Chronicles 16:34; Psalm 119:12–18; Luke 1:46–55

The Promises of Motherhood

ABUNDANCE: 1 Kings 17:16; John 10:10; 2 Corinthians 9:6

COMPASSION: Genesis 21:16–19; 29:31–35; Psalm 86:15; 145:9; Isaiah 49:15–16; Lamentations 3:22–24; Luke 7:13–16; 2 Corinthians 1:3–4

DELIVERANCE: Exodus 33:14; Psalm 3:8; 18:1–3; 34:3–4, 18–20; 72:12

FRUITFULNESS: Proverbs 31:30–31; John 15:5, 15–17; 2 Corinthians 9:10; Colossians 1:9–11

GRACE: Psalm 84:11; Luke 1:50; Galatians 1:3–4; Romans 3:23–24; 5:17

GUIDANCE: Psalm 32:8; 48:14; Isaiah 30:21; 49:3; 58:11; Luke 12:12; John 16:13

HONOR: Exodus 20:12; Ruth 3:11; Psalm 8:4–5; 91:14–16; Proverbs 11:16; Matthew 19:19; Luke 1:46–55

JOY: Psalm 16:11; 30:4–6; 118:24; Luke 1:14; John 15:10–12; 16:23–24

LOVE: Psalm 5:11–12; John 3:16;13:34–35; Romans 5:8; 8:28, 34–39

PROSPERITY: 1 Kings 17:14–16; 2 Kings 4:2–7; Psalm 1:2–3; Luke 6:38

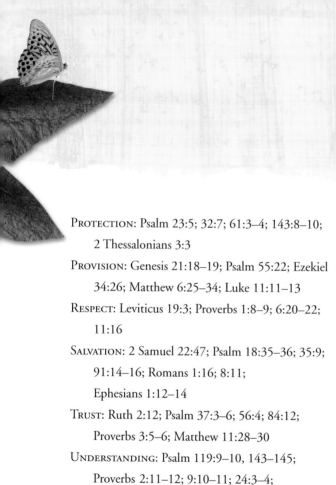

PROTECTION: Psalm 23:5; 32:7; 61:3–4; 143:8–10;
   2 Thessalonians 3:3

PROVISION: Genesis 21:18–19; Psalm 55:22; Ezekiel
   34:26; Matthew 6:25–34; Luke 11:11–13

RESPECT: Leviticus 19:3; Proverbs 1:8–9; 6:20–22;
   11:16

SALVATION: 2 Samuel 22:47; Psalm 18:35–36; 35:9;
   91:14–16; Romans 1:16; 8:11;
   Ephesians 1:12–14

TRUST: Ruth 2:12; Psalm 37:3–6; 56:4; 84:12;
   Proverbs 3:5–6; Matthew 11:28–30

UNDERSTANDING: Psalm 119:9–10, 143–145;
   Proverbs 2:11–12; 9:10–11; 24:3–4;
   Ephesians 1:18–19; 1 John 5:20

Notes

Grateful acknowledgment is given
to Elly Preston of The Purple Door
for the use of her jewelry in the design of
this book. To view the full line of her
beautiful creations, go to
www.mypurpledoor.com.